TEN
Stories

Julius Rockwell

Published in honor and in memory of
Julius Rockwell

ISBN: 978-0-9907428-4-5
Printed in the United States
Cover image © Belinka/Shutterstock
Book design: Vered R. Mares

For copies, please contact
VP&D House, Inc.
1352 W. 25th Ave.
Anchorage, Alaska 99503
www.vpdhouse.com • info@vpdhouse.com
907-720-7559

Contents

My Early Childhood (1920–1923)

I was born on July 25, 1918, at 6 Spring Street, Taunton, Massachusetts, to Alice Hearne and Julius Rockwell, being the first of three children, all boys. I was named Julius Rockwell Jr. having two Julius Rockwell's before me. I lived in this house on Spring Street until I was five years old and we all moved with my two younger brothers to Andover, Massachusetts.

During the summers my father would leave us at West Harwich, on Cape Cod. My first two summers were spent in a white cottage, and the second two summers in a green cottage.

My earliest memories are from my first summer at the white cottage, which was the summer I turned two. I remember that because my brother Bill, who was a year younger, was too small to do anything with me.

My first memory was beautiful. The cottage was on a macadam road that ran along a bluff overlooking the water. A young preteen, Mary Vieira, worked as nanny for our family, and had me walk with her to the grocery store. We turned left out of the cottage, went down the road to the corner of a street, and then we turned left again and cut across a vacant corner lot to another road, which led to the grocery store. On the way across the lot, I found a Queen Anne's Lace, a composite flower. It was about two and a half feet tall, just my height. Without damaging the flower, I held it in my hands and gazed down into the hundreds of its tiny blossoms. There were three small insects crawling around among them, a red one, a black one and a brown and black one. I remember that looking at it made me feel so good, because I saw it as an illustration of life as I knew it. I have total recall of this experience, to this day. The tiny blossoms were each connected to each other the way we are, all coming from the same root. I had been taught about relationships, by having five uncles on my father's side, four aunts and an uncle on my mother's side and many cousins. Thus, I already knew that I, too, like each little blossom was connected to many.

While walking down that hot road back from the grocery store, I often found toads, which had been run over, flattened by cars and dried in the sun. I felt sorry for them, so I snuck them into my pockets, took them back and hid them under our cottage where it was cool and moist. I hoped they would revive in such a place. Even at that age I realized that it would be unwise to reveal my experiment to adults. My mother was distressed when she discovered some forgotten toads in my pockets while doing the wash. Possibly she intervened in my activities the following year, because I did not do this during my second year there. I don't remember much else about my first year at the white cottage.

I remember playing with my brother, Bill during the second year in the white cottage. We often played with the Bent girls, Peggy and Harriet. Between our two houses was a field that seemed very large to us, where a grass grew that was almost as fine as hair. I have never seen anything like it anywhere else. It was about a foot or two high and when the wind blew it formed waves across the field. We all loved to roll in this grass and often did so.

We had at least another adventure during one of those summers in the white cottage. I loved to eat swordfish and nearby there was a dock where the swordfish boats tied up. My father arranged for the family to take a trip on one of these. It had a broad bowsprit with handrails on each side. A fisherman would go out on this to harpoon a swordfish. One time I snuck out onto the bowsprit, only to be quickly retrieved by my mother. She always kept a sharp eye out for me because of my adventuresome ways.

The next two summers were spent in the green cottage. This cottage was much larger than the white cottage and my mother invited many relatives to it, often to stay for several days or weeks. Some of the guests had children of our age. Thus, we were exposed to many different family cultures. My memory of that time was spotty, however, I do remember a number of small incidents.

We were spanked when we were naughty, by whoever was handy. This was always done with a bare hand on our buttocks. One of our guests, Jack, had especially large hands. My brother and I nicknamed him, "Jack, the Spanking Man." He seemed to like this and would often show us how big his hands were. He never actually did spank us, but we were particularly good when he was around!

The Green Cottage was in a pinewood, close to a bluff overlooking a beach. Nearby was a path to a stairway, used by many, that led down to the beach. My brother and I would go there and play. We were not swimmers, but someone had given me some water wings, which if I blew up would float me. By watching dogs swim, I had learned to dog paddle. I noticed a raft some distance from shore with a person on it and felt that it would be a good destination. Out I went. The waves were about two feet high, so I was out of sight at least half the time. When I reached the raft and climbed up it's ladder, the woman sunbathing on it looked surprised and asked me where I had come from. I nonchalantly replied that I had just swum there. I lay down and sunbathed, too. After a while I got up and walked around on the raft. My mother came down the stairs to the beach and saw me there. I waved to her. She called out that I should come back right away. I did. I did not do that again, but now I knew, that I could!

My father would come down on the weekends and during his vacation times. My brother and I were always happy when he came because he took us on many adventures. For instance, one time he took the whole family on a canoe trip to Monomoy Point. The tide was low and the water, clear and shallow. We could look down and see small scallops the size of a silver dollar, swimming about. We would pick them up and eat them

7

raw. I remember sitting in the bottom of the canoe, reaching over and picking up several by myself. They were delicious. Sadly, we cannot do this anymore because the Bay has become polluted.

Living in the green cottage was quite informal. Normally my brother and I had our own little table and chairs for our meals that our mother would fix. When we had guests we ate at the big table with them, so we could learn things by listening. Once when my mother's father was visiting, my brother Bill was sitting very low on a chair because he was quite small. When he chewed, his lower jaw would hit his plate and tilt it. My grandfather ran up the stairs and brought down a huge dictionary. He lifted Bill from his seat, put the dictionary on the chair, and put him back down on the dictionary. Now Bill's head was close to the same level as ours at the table. My mother was very impressed by this and wondered why my father had not thought of it.

It was in the green cottage that I learned that boys were different from girls. The Bent children were visiting and I saw Peggy, who was only two, quite naked. This was how I discovered that girls do not have a penis. I now felt rather sorry for girls because a penis was so convenient. It would be hard for them to make a good mark on the snow. At that time, and for this reason, I felt that girls were inferior to boys. Since then I have learned much better.

It was also at the green cottage that I learned about my mother's social values. She was particular with whom we mixed. There was a woman living nearby who my mother did not think was very nice. However, she had a radio and had invited us children over to hear music. Not many people had radios then, including us. Classical music was on daily between 5 PM and 6 PM. Although my mother was not keen on letting us spend time with this lady, she let us go over to hear the music, as long as we came straight home afterwards. We enjoyed these visits and the cookies given to us.

This is all I can remember about my early life in West Harwich.

Our house on 6 Spring Street, Taunton, Massachusetts, was an old house, even in those days. The house was on a narrow lot and it went way back from the street. The stables were attached to the house, but were no longer used for horses. Someone had once told me that houses were no longer designed this way because rats from the stables could easily get into the house. Cars were sometimes parked in the stables. My father used rented or borrowed cars and my mother did not drive.

The house had a nice front porch with steps leading up from the sidewalk. The porch had a couch and chairs on it and was overhung by the bedrooms above. We would sit on the couch and watch people walking by in the evening. If we knew them we would invite them to come and sit with us. The front door opened into a long hall. As you went in, there was a parlor on the immediate right, into which I was not supposed to go. It was kept immaculate and ready for tea at all times. People dropped by in those days without warning. The dining room was behind the parlor. On the left was the living room where, I was welcome. The kitchen was behind the living room and further back, stairs led to the second floor and the bedrooms. The attic was above these.

As I have mentioned, I was not supposed to go into the parlor, but one day I went in with a group of guests who were being shown around. I saw a huge mirror, which made a big impression on me. Later, I often snuck into the parlor because I loved that mirror. My relatives would look at me and say, "He has Henry's nose", "He has Lawrence's eyes", "He has Francis's chin", and so on. This made me nervous because at that age I thought these people might want their features back. But alone in the room I could look into this mirror and see that they were *my* nose, *my* eyes, *my* chin. This gave me a great deal of comfort and reassurance.

I later learned that this huge, five by six foot mirror came from the Paris World's Fair of 1889. My father had picked it up during his grand tour in 1900, when the buildings of the Fair were being demolished. Somehow, he brought it back and put it in this house, in Taunton, that he had bought in 1917. When we moved from here to Andover, Massachusetts, in 1923 there was no room for the mirror in the house that we rented. The mirror was put in the home of my Uncle Francis. He had a nice big house in North Andover, about four miles away,

In 1928, my father rented the farmhouse on Arden Farm. There was no room for the mirror in this house either. However, while we were here, my uncle Francis was committed to an asylum and his house was sold. Consequently, the mirror had to be moved and so it was put in a crate and stored in our garage on Arden Farm. There it stayed until after my parents moved away. My father rented this farmhouse for forty years and after he and my mother finally moved, the garage, was torn down. Lewis, who was a co-worker of my son John, on the estate, said he had put the mirror in a safe place when the garage was torn down. Years later Lewis told John that he had sold the mirror, but we were never sure about this. Eventually the farm passed on to the owner's son and after he died it went to his widow, Roslyn Wood.

My parents died in the late 1960s and early 70s and it wasn't until 2006 that the widow, Roslyn, kindly let us know that she had found the crated mirror when she was clearing out the unused stable. She recalled that several years before, my mother had kept asking her about the mirror. When I heard the news that the long lost mirror had been found, I was thrilled. My sons, John and Bill, made the proper arrangements with Christie's, in Boston, and had it carefully shipped to me. Now, I can look into this long-lost family mirror and see who I am and so can others who visit me in my condo.

In Taunton my parents' bedroom was upstairs over the front porch. Also upstairs there was also a guest bedroom, a bedroom for my brother Bill and I, a nursery and a bathroom. When I was sick I was put in the guest bedroom. I remember on one occasion after I had had my tonsils removed, that I vomited blood into a little crescent shaped bowl. It fascinated me that I could do this without dying.

The guest bedroom was large and it was also used as a "children's living room" and reading room. It was here that I remember people reading stories to us. We were told many stories, but there were two that were important to me; one was the classical legend of 'Horatius at the Bridge' and the other was 'Peter Pan'.

Horatius was a Roman warrior of great renown. In this story I remember that he defended Rome from the invading Etruscan army. To enter Rome, the Etruscans had to cross the River Tiber. The bridge over the River Tiber was narrow, with no railings at the sides. It was the only way the enemy could get across the river. Horatius stood on the middle of the bridge with his sword and shield and would not let any of the Etruscan soldiers pass him to enter Rome. He either killed them or knocked them into the river. This went on for at least half a day until his army was able to destroy the bridge. He then swam back across the Tiber to Rome. Thus, one warrior stopped a whole army single-handed. I was very impressed that one person alone could turn history.

Regarding the 'Peter Pan' story, there was an incident in which my parents told me that I had once fallen out of the second story window of the guest's bedroom and landed in the fern bed. I do not remember this at all. However, the reason I bring this up is because although I don't remember the incident, I do remember the effect it had on me. It must have been after I heard the story of Peter Pan in which Tinker Bell tells Peter Pan and Wendy that we can fly if we really want to. An adult whom I liked and in whom I had faith, had told this story to me, and so I tried to fly out of the second story window. I am basing this on the evidence of my own personality, and the fact that I had chills for many years every time Peter Pan was mentioned in conversation. From then on, and even to this day, I have difficulty in trusting other people's judgment.

We would often sit on our front porch and watch what went by on the street. One day the local Masons paraded by in their uniforms with a band. Their uniform consisted of kilts. I had heard the story of the 'Emperor's New Clothes', in which a shrewd tailor had made the vain Emperor an imaginary suit from 'expensive fabric'. According to the tailor the suit was magic and could not be seen by anyone who was incompetent to do his work. No man, including the Emperor, who had paid lavishly for the suit, wanted to admit that they could not see it. The Emperor arranged for a big parade in which he could display his new suit. A small child watching the parade, unconcerned about *his* competence, called out, "The Emperor isn't wearing any clothes!" Everyone realized the truth, and the Emperor was furious. The tailor had already been paid and was nowhere to be found.

Knowing this story, when I saw the kilts, I yelled out at the top of my voice, "They don't have any pants on!" much to the amusement of all around.

It was curious to me why adults would try to encourage romance for very small children, regardless of how the children felt. I remember one incident in which I was with a number of children sitting on the steps of a front porch. I must have been about three at the time. Sitting next to me was a little two-year-old girl. One of the ladies watching over us asked me to kiss the girl. I did not think much of girls at that time. I looked at the child having no desire to kiss her at all, and she looked at me as though she did not want to be kissed. We both sat there for a moment, and then looking over at her curiously, I noticed a puddle seeping quietly onto the step from under her dress.

"The Eye of God."

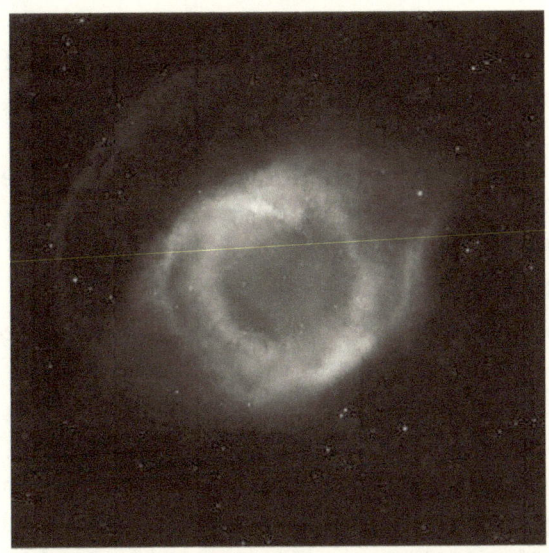

"AWESOME! This photo is a very rare one, taken by NASA. This kind of event occurs once in 3000 years. This photo has done miracles in many lives. Make a wish. You have looked at the eye of God. Surely you will see the changes in your life within a day."

Next to our house was a church. We were not involved in it, but it was there. I must have been about three or four years old at the time and I had an inquisitive friend who was a big guy, possibly as old as five. He had found a way that we could crawl into the church through a small hole in the basement. We did. Both of us liked to explore. We went up into the empty nave, which was big and awesome. Over the altar was a beautiful, huge stained-glass window showing a huge eye. It appeared to be looking directly into our souls. "What is that?" I asked. "Oh that's the Eye of God", my friend answered. "He can look right into your mind and soul with it and know everything you are thinking and would like to do." The idea made me feel very uneasy. I had always supposed that my own thoughts, dreams and desires were known only to me. This news was very disquieting. I rapidly made an inventory of all my undesirable thoughts. The fact that I had enjoyed sneaking into this church was paramount. I asked my friend if this were true only in the presence of that eye. He told me that the stained-glass window was just a picture of the real thing. The true Eye of God was everywhere and there was no escaping it.

Since then I have strived to have only thoughts that were okay with God and avoid dwelling on evil things, at least eighty percent of the time. Interestingly enough, I found the following quote in the journal, 'Science': "Live the journey, not the destination. This is not a dress rehearsal!"

When I was in Taunton I had a friend named George Reed. He was a big guy and must have been all of six years old! I was about four years old. This was during the time that I was having 'Horatio at the Bridge' read to me and I felt very martial. George and I liked making things. We concentrated on making bows and arrows. I remember how he also taught me that apple wood was the best material from which to make a bow, because it was bendable and springy. There was an apple tree near by and so we had plenty of good material for making bows. We made some good bows with string and apple branches. However, we had less success with our arrows, because we couldn't find enough feathers to make steady flights. George Reed made a big impression on me. He taught me that I could make things.

In a factory courtyard near where I lived, large empty boxes appeared from time to time. We were allowed to take them, and so we did. We would carry them to someone's driveway and here we would play with them. One of the leader kids invited 'good guys' to get under an over turned box and sit in the darkness. At times there were as many as six of us little 'good guys' squeezed in under a box. The leader would bring a flash light bulb and battery and use nails to create a circuit to make the bulb light up. This was fascinating to me and started my interest in electricity and physics.

Sometimes my father would take me in a canoe on the Taunton River. We would paddle up the river until we came to an island and on the island was an ancient stone tower. The tower had been there long before the first settlers came to this area. Legend had it, that it had been built by the Norsemen who had come to this country, and they had named the area Vinland, because of the great wild grapes there. I wondered what these people were like, but nobody could tell me. No one seemed to know.

We could walk to Kindergarten from home. We would go past the factory that had the boxes, then across a bridge, over a greasy river and finally over a big street. The Kindergarten occupied a large lot with plenty of room for playing outside.

On the way to Kindergarten one day when we were crossing the bridge over the greasy river, I asked my chaperone who was caring for us, what the name of it was. She said it was the Great Green Greasy Limpopo River. This did not seem right to me because I thought the Limpopo River was in Africa and somehow I knew that this was not Africa. I felt unhappy because there was so much garbage and oil in the river. I knew this had to be bad for the fish and should not be allowed. I thought when I grew up maybe I could help clean up rivers. In fact, later in Alaska, I did work with the Anchorage Waterways Council, doing just that.

All I remember about my Kindergarten experience is that we had assignments to do in class and if we did not finish them, we had to stay in during recess to work on them. If I finished my assignments early I was allowed to spend the rest of recess cleaning the blackboards. I can remember staying in during recesses all the time. I have always admired superlative people and I feel that I was one of the superlative people because I flunked out of Kindergarten. Towards the end of my second year of Kindergarten I was still flunking, but I was very happy that we moved away to Andover, Massachusetts, where they did not have a Kindergarten at that time.

My father owned a piece of land in Wareham, Massachusetts, which was not far away from Taunton. On this land he had a cabin in which he lived before he had bought the house on Spring Street. It was still furnished and we went out on one occasion to pick up some of his belongings. We looked in the bottom drawer of the bureau and there we found a wood mouse's nest full of mice that scurried away. I asked my father what they were and he said, "That's Whitefoot, the Wood Mouse and his family". 'Whitefoot', was the name of one of the characters from Thornton Burgess' children's stories. He did not disturb their nest.

On the west boundary of the lot was a stream. The man who owned the opposite side of the stream had put a board in the water to divert the current over to my father's side where it was eroding the bank and adding to the land on the neighbor's side. I advised my father, to take that plank out of the stream. He said it was his neighbor's board, so I told him to take it and put it on the neighbor's land. My father agreed with me and did just that.

On some Sundays we would take the trolley out to the end of the line, to Whittington. We took a picnic basket and blanket, walked three quarters of a mile, spread out the blanket and had a nice picnic beside a beautiful lake.

At Christmas time we would go down from Taunton to visit my mother's parents in Wayne, Pennsylvania. This was a very interesting trip. We would have a friend drive us by car from Taunton to Fall River. There we got on a boat and slept in berths in a stateroom. We woke up the next morning tied up to the dock in New York City. We would catch a train from here to Philadelphia and then switch to another train, which would take us to Wayne, Pennsylvania. My grandfather, Hearne, would pick us up in his car and drive us to his house. It was a huge house built very strongly and would hold several families.

When we arrived at my grandfather's house there were usually a number of my mother's sisters and some of their children there. It was fun to play with our cousins, which were about our age. The food, or course was marvelous. I also re-member the time that I tried to smoke with my cousins. We did this behind a couch. My grandfather caught us, and ignoring the fact that we were smoking, told us that we should not be playing with matches behind couches. We did not try that again.

During one of our trips to Wayne, my mother bought a Scottish terrier puppy, to take back to Andover. She found out that dogs were not allowed in the train's coaches. They had to be kept in a cage in the baggage room. Not liking this idea, my mother put the little puppy, which she named Sarah, into a picnic basket and smuggled her aboard the train. She told us it was a secret. The conductor for the train, who seemed older than my father, was a very nice man. He chatted with us boys and treated us like grownups. We asked him if he could keep a secret. He said he could. We lifted the lid of the picnic basket and showed him the puppy. He looked at it and then looked at my mother, who was horrified. Laughing, he put the lid down on the picnic basket, told us not to show it to anybody else and went on down the carriage. That taught me that there are some very nice people in the world. While younger people know the rules, older people know when they can bend them.

The Bicycle

I was six years old when we moved from Taunton to Highland Road in Andover, Massachusetts. I had a small bicycle with eighteen-inch wheels, big tires and no coastal brake. When I went down hill I would put my feet on the handlebars and coast. The roads in those days were covered with ashes from the furnaces that burnt soft coal. The dust from these ashes was full of multi-pointed little grains, about an eighth of an inch in diameter.

When I coasted down a hill on my bicycle the chain sometimes jammed. The back wheel would stop and I would go head over heals. I remember, on one particular occasion, this happened when I was wearing short trousers and as I rolled down the hill, my knees became imbedded with little pieces of coal dust ashes. I was crying when I came home and my mother did what she could to extricate as many pieces of the sharp ashes from my knees as possible. It was quite painful. I continued to use this little bicycle until I could buy a larger one. I even remember riding it to church one winter day when the snow was about ten inches deep. It was a valiant little devise.

The following summer I resolved to get a better bicycle with a coastal brake. I went through all the material I could find on bicycles and picked out one called, 'The Reading Standard'. It had 28inch wheels, and the tires had inner tubes. I also planned to buy a two speed coastal brake, for two dollars from Sears and Roebuck. At a total of forty dollars, this was more than I could afford right away, so I had to save up my money. I earned money doing odd jobs for five cents an hour, and asked everybody to give me Christmas and birthday presents in cash only. Some of my family members were very generous with their gifts. I remember once getting a five-dollar bill. By the time I reached fourth grade I was able to buy my blue and white, Reading Standard bicycle. It was large for me at the time, but I could manage.

I used my new bike all the way through High School and then took it to college with me. Once in 1937, I rode it from Ann Arbor, Michigan, to Andover, Massachusetts. For this trip I purchased anti leak fluid for my tires, a couple of rolls of electric tape and an odometer, to see how far I was going each day. The tape was used to wrap the tires onto the wheel rims, so that they did not fly off when I went down mountain roads. I got quite a write-up in three local newspapers for this 806-mile, ten-day trip.

I used my Reading Standard bike to get around town when I was at college in Ann Arbor. It had two speeds, high and low, but I never seemed to use the lower speed. I found it safest to go at the speed of the traffic, which was about thirty miles an hour. One day, I was traveling at this speed along side a bus, while passing a row of parked cars on my right. Suddenly the driver of a parked car ahead of me opened his door. Trying to avoid it caused me to lean against the bus for an instant. There was just enough room between the bus and his door, for me to squeeze through. I hit them both, but somehow succeeded to get between them without falling.

In 1940 when I graduated from college, I left my bicycle in Michigan. Much later, in 1985 when I was on a visit to Ann Arbor, I was delighted to see my old friend, Bill Strauch, riding my dependable Reading Standard.

The Cabbage Story

My brother Bill and I were both at the University of Michigan together between 1937 and 1940. At that time students were not allowed to have automobiles. They were not necessary because everything we needed was within walking distance.

We lived in a co-operative house. Students rented co-operative houses for a very reasonable room-rate. We shared the work of running the house, which included preparing our own meals. Most houses had about thirty selected members, twenty of who lived in the house and thirty of whom just ate there. A number of houses joined together to form The Inter-Cooperative Council. Bill was the purchasing agent for the Council and because of this the University gave him special permission to use a car for picking up food at the market in Detroit. His car happened to be a hearse, which he had bought for the reasonable price of fifty dollars!

Bill's procedure was to go into Detroit with an assistant and visit the Farmer's Markets in the late afternoon. He would spend some time in Detroit and then return to the markets close to their midnight closing time, because the farmers would drop their prices just before going home.

Bill and his assistant, Ginsberg, had time to kill between going to downtown Detroit and the farmers markets, and they spent that time at random, which sometimes included visiting pawn shops. One night, Bill, who was tall and gaunt, picked up an old fashioned undertaker's outfit. He acquired a somewhat disheveled tall silk hat, an old fashioned coat with long tails, an appropriately buttoned white shirt and a wooden cane with a death-head handle. His assistant, Ginsberg, who was short and chubby, was similarly attired, but with a derby hat.

At buying time Bill and Ginsberg would go into the farmers' markets to look at the food and prices. If they saw interesting items, Bill would point at them with his cane and Ginsberg would ask how much the farmer would be prepared to drop the price. Ginsberg would write this down and they would move on to something else, since they were checking stuff from several markets. When it was getting late they would start to buy, usually by then at a low offering price. On the particular day in question, the bottom had dropped out of the cabbage market. Apparently all the farmers had brought in their cabbages and they were able to buy many bushel baskets at a penny a head. Bill and Ginsberg, who had both had a few beers, went wild at this price. The cabbages were dumped into the back of the hearse.

On the way back to Ann Arbor from Detroit, there was a 40-mile, four lane divided highway to Ypsilanti. The hearse had no top speed. It picked-up slowly, but then went faster and faster. They went barreling down the road at about 65 mph, when an Irish policeman stopped them. "You are going pretty fast," he said. My brother, making sure that the death-head cane was visible said, "We have come a long way and have a long way to go." Ginsberg said, "And we have much work to do." The policeman looked at the hearse, suddenly became quite pale and said, "Go ahead!"

When Bill and Ginsberg reached Ypsilanti they stopped at a special 24-hour restaurant to get their customary five-cent hamburger. They did not understand why the policeman let them go. Getting out of the hearse they looked at it they way he did. The wind was blowing just the same way and it parted the curtains in one of the windows. There, close to the window, was a cabbage head with black spots, which looked just like a face. Behind this cabbage was another similar one and with the headlights reflecting in from the other side, it made it appear that there were countless heads piled in the hearse.

This happy tale of purchase was marred only by the fact that the co-operative members from all the houses, ate nothing but cabbage for three weeks, but had to enjoy coleslaw, corned beef with cabbage, and boiled cabbage!

The Fudge Theory

After my junior year at college I had a summer job as a camp counselor at Camp Winniecook in Unity, Maine. Ed Rand, the owner's son, a young bachelor of many extraordinary talents, managed the camp. He was inclined to give me advice on many aspects of my life and was a brilliant and creative young man.

In the summer of 1939 Ed asked me how I did with the ladies. I told him that I took them to the movies and dancing about once a week. He asked me how I felt about them. I told him I had a vague feeling of wanting to be with them and that this feeling was difficult to define. He asked me if I had an objective with them. I said not exactly. I just wanted to be with them. I would invite them to do things with me that I thought they might like to do. He replied that I would get nowhere that way and that I needed to have an objective with them. To accomplish anything, he said, I needed to have an objective. He cited Hitler who wanted all of Europe but set an objective of getting just one piece at a time. This he could do and did.

If I did not know my objective with the ladies, Ed told me, I should make one up, being better to have a fake one than none at all. I asked him what he had in mind. He answered, "Take something simple and direct. For instance, get them to make you some fudge. If you can get them to make you some fudge, you can probably get them to do anything you want." I asked him, "If one made me some fudge and I still did not have a better objective, then what should I do? He said that I should learn about fudge. There is no perfect fudge. Some is too sugary; some is too gooey; some lacks nuts, raisins or little gummy things, etc. The point was to keep her trying to please me until I was ready to move on. For a 20-year-old this idea seemed full of desirable possibilities. As a camp counselor my options were quite limited. In my senior year in college, I needed to get all A's to make up for my low average, so instead of taking on a new idea I decided to stick to dancing and taking my ladies to the movies.

After college was the Navy, where I thought things would be different. It was amazing. Remembering Ed's advise, I asked for fudge but received nearly everything except fudge. For instance, there was an attractive woman whom I often took dancing. Whenever I took her to the 'Top of the Mark' (Hopkins Hotel) in San Francisco and we started dancing, the band would automatically play, "Don't throw bouquets at me." She asked me what she could do for me, and I said, "My dear, please make me some fudge." She said, "Are you sure you want fudge? Okay, then, fudge it will be." Later, she made me brownies. I received brownies, pies, chocolate layer cake, tarts, cookies, etc., but no fudge. My friend Ed was right when he said, "It is not as easy as it sounds." Six years in the Navy and no fudge.

At the end of the war, I went to the University of Washington to study fisheries. My friend and roommate, Christopher and I rented an apartment right next to campus. Christopher had a girlfriend, Ellie Masters, the daughter of a famous Broadway actress. She was going to the School of Drama, which was nearby. Ellie and a friend of hers studied in our apartment nearly every afternoon because it was convenient for them. Ellie felt my beautiful feisty Norwegian lady friend was not good enough for me and that the woman with whom she studied would be much better. I had never met this person because I was at work when they studied in the afternoons. Her friend had to go home for dinner across town at 5 PM. Chris and I never saw her because we both worked and came home at 6 PM. Then, generally, a group of us ate at a little Greek restaurant on the Avenue. Conversations varied and of course, I explained about the Fudge Theory in considerable detail. Ellie liked this and thought the theory was hilarious.

When summer came, Chris, I, and two others were sent to Alaska to study the environment of the salmon that spawned there. We made these studies on several carefully selected pristine streams isolated from most human activity. We traveled to them in small skiffs.

Bell Island Hot Springs was chosen as our headquarters. Bell Island is located in Behm Canal and is about 75 miles northeast of Ketchikan. It was a "historical resort" at the time we stayed there. The warm springs were wonderful. In a special building there were large stone tubs. The tubs were deep and long enough for one to lie in full length and be completely covered with water. Each tub had three pipes with wooden plugs: one for draining, one with very hot water from the springs and one with cold water from the stream. It was easy to regulate the temperature and keep it just right.

Bell Island Hot Springs had its heyday before inside plumbing was installed in homes in Ketchikan. People would come out there and get a nice, easy hot bath. The owner had built cabins so visitors could stay as long as they liked, also a general store so they could buy food and other tourist's needs. He established a post office because mail was the primary means of communication. The island had its own stream that had salmon and trout in profusion with a nice trail beside it. It was very easy to fish. At the time of our visit, only trawlers and other fisherman used the place to get a warm bath and pick up mail and food. We were able to rent the one usable cabin as our home base. It had no leaks and four large rooms on two floors. One room had a stove. We were remote, isolated and secure.

On the way up to Ketchikan we all decided to grow beards. This was a hazardous process for me because during the early stages the hair on my face reminded observers of a movie star whose role was torturing people in horror movies. Once in a bar, someone tried to attack me for this reason. My friends got me out of there. The full-grown beard turned out to be quite handsome.

On the job we worked in pairs, and used two small skiffs to go out to our streams. One day when we returned, one of the two ladies that ran the place brought up a package that had come in the mail. It was addressed to me from Ellie and her friend. It was 8 inches long, 4 inches high, and 5 inches wide. We opened it immediately and of course. It was fudge! Not only that, but it was exceptional fudge, just the right consistency, not too sugary and not too gooey. It had crumbled nuts in it, it had tiny raisins and it had little gummy things in it. It was beyond belief! To thank the two young women for the fudge, I wrote up a   description of one of our adventures we called "The High Tide," but that is another story.

On our return to Seattle, my Norwegian friend was absolutely nonplussed by my beard.   Apparently she liked to read the emotions on my face. This was impossible now, even though it was a nice black beard and I had it well trimmed.

I went to Michigan the following week to be best man at my brother Frank's wedding. I was surprised to learn how different cultures were in 1947. In Seattle beards were occasionally seen and taken in stride. But in Michigan nobody had beards and the presence of mine brought pandemonium. On one occasion while out walking, a kind but unknown person, half a block away yelled directions to the closest barbershop. Socially, all conversations would stop if I entered a room of twenty guests. A few actually liked my beard. However, I contemplated cutting it off because I did not want to steal the show from the bride on her wedding day. My New York uncle, a professor at The Union Theological Seminary, who was marrying the couple, begged me to keep the beard. He had had one once and had regretted cutting it off. But the attention it got was so strong that I decided to cut mine. My new sister-in-law thanked me after the wedding.

On returning to Seattle, I found that my Norwegian lady friend was greatly relieved to see my beard gone. Ellie said that the time had come for me to meet her friend and thank her for the fudge. Being in the School of Drama, they had to do everything just right.

In the University District of Seattle 'The Avenue' ran parallel to the University Campus. The little Greek Restaurant, the

School of Drama, and our apartment were all on it. Also, on the Avenue was a small teashop, a favorite for young women. It was always full in the afternoon. Ellie told Chris to meet her there at three o'clock. She told me to accompany him. We were to go to the teashop, enter and look around in a lost way, at all the full tables. We would see Ellie and her friend sitting at a table with two empty chairs. Ellie would invite us to join them. The rest was up to us.

Everything worked as planned and I found myself sitting beside the most beautiful woman I had ever seen. I had to arrange to see that person again, and again, and again. My interest in my Norwegian lady faded away. Here was a woman who made me the perfect fudge without ever having seen me.

We were married in four months!

Pre Hit Day

In October 1941, on my first trip to Pearl Harbor, I was on the USS Tangier. I thought about the imminence of war. The Japanese were moving towards and taking over the Philippines and Indonesia with all its oil. I expected the Pearl Harbor community to be alert and ready for battle. Somewhat to my dismay I found that it was the upcoming Christmas holiday season that was being anticipated.

I reported on board the USS Lexington CV2, and received my quarters and living instructions. The Lexington was tied up at Pearl Harbor, Naval Air Station on Oahu. I was assigned to the junior officer's mess where I ate and socialized. Surprisingly, the major topic of conversation was not the imminence of Japanese aggression but rather, who should be taken to the next dance.

On hearing that I was in Hawaii, my mother told me to be sure to look up a college classmate of hers, Ikki Irwin. Ikki was half Japanese and half American and was married to a big plantation owner on the north side of Oahu. Soon after arriving at Pearl Harbor I called Ikki Irwin's household. She was on the mainland, but her husband cordially invited me to come over for dinner and sent a vehicle to pick me up.

Our conversation was fascinating. He was under the impression that the Japanese would be taking over the Hawaiian Islands, and his main desire was to be among the Americans who would help them do so. In this way he felt he could ensure the likelihood of his family keeping his plantation. I was appalled by this, being out here with my shipmates and other friends, to risk our lives and prevent that very thing from happening. I had read about this out-look before, where inhabitants of an occupied country were more loyal to their families than their country. He saw this disagreement in me and suggested that I would probably be more interested in finding a girlfriend than in helping the Japanese. He gave me the name and number of a girl called Anne Morgan, suggesting that I might like to take her out. It turned out that Anne Morgan was the daughter of the former Queen of the Hawaiian nation and J.P. Morgan, the famous tycoon who owned most of the Islands. We had several dates and my roommate claims that she was not interested in nations or companies, but mostly in the pleasures of being a woman. However, I realized that she did not appeal to me.

On the Lexington, I fell in with two other young officers. One night we visited a top, posh, nightclub, featuring the best hula dancers on the Island. Arriving at this place at about eight o'clock, I looked across the room and saw one of the most beautiful women I had ever seen, sitting at a table with a man. I admired her to my friends. One of them jumped on me verbally, ridiculing my opinion saying, "You know nothing about her. She may be some sluttish undesirable type that you would not invite into your house." I felt physically hurt by his remarks because subconsciously I had already imagined this woman as my close friend. I responded angrily that he had no business talking that way about my 'dear friend'. The shipmate who had made the insulting remarks looked at me whimsically and said, "You are angry, aren't you, defending a person you have never met." There was a pause as the enormity of my foolishness set in. I thought to myself, she is obviously the girl of my dreams, seen from half way across the room. I realized the unlikeliness of anything coming of it. My friend, who was insulting her, chuckled. "She is my cousin!" He said. For me the emotional charge was full of static, which he read in my face and body language. He continued on and explained that he and his cousin each corresponded with different family members to get news from home. To share the news they ate together about once a month. Their next monthly meeting on December 5th was coming up in a week or two. He said, "You guys come in here at about eight o'clock on the 5th. All the tables will be filled but we will have a table for four. Come in looking for a seat with a lost look until you spot us. When you catch our eye, wave. I will wave back and invite you guys over to our table. The rest will be up to you."

During this interim period I busied myself in learning my duties, studying the ship and thinking about the upcoming date with internal excitement continually rising.

Finally December fifth came. At noon I was thinking very much about the date, but at two thirty in the afternoon, word came over the loudspeaker, "All departments make ready for getting underway!" This was absolutely unheard of. Nobody ever sailed out of peacetime Pearl Harbor on a Friday afternoon. But orders are orders and get ready we did. We left port late in the afternoon and headed south escorted by three cruisers and six destroyers, having been told that our target practice had been poor recently and that we needed more of it. We in Engineering thought that this was an unlikely story.

My first war duty on a fighting ship was quite exciting to me. I was assigned as the Junior Electrical Officer to assist the Electrical Officer. Adjusting to the details of living and performing military activities was totally absorbing.

Two days later at about seven in the morning, we were called to General Quarters. It was unprecedented to have General Quarters on a Sunday morning. Once there, we were told to sit down. The Captain on the loud speaker explained what was happening in Pearl Harbor, which was a full and very destructive attack by the Japanese. Somewhat belatedly on December 7th 1941, war was declared. The ship's task force needed to plan for an unanticipated course of action. I learned from the Assistant Navigator, another junior officer with access to knowledge not received by Engineering that our Task Force was going to attack the Marshal Islands in retaliation. I asked the Assistant Navigator, "What do they have there?" He answered, "Not much, just a single airfield, a hundred or so airplanes and a garrison of about 500 men."

"When was that information obtained", I asked dubiously, having read recently in Time Magazine how the Japanese had rapidly been building up its resources in the Marshal Islands. "1932" came the answer.

All of us felt rather uneasy as we started towards the Marshals. Apparently others also doubted the value of this estimate of Japanese strength. A day or two later we received word from a submarine who had checked out the Islands. They reported: six airfields, each with 500 planes, and vastly improved garrisons containing over 2,500 men. An attack by our small Task Force would have been suicide, so the attack was called off.

In those days, Navy tankers refueled ships that were out for any length of time. This operation required that the two ships were heading into the wind along side each other. However, this could not work here because the waves generated by the wind were coming from head on and waves from a previous storm were coming from the side. The result was that the two ships were clashing with each other and the tanker's cranes were punching holes into the Lexington's stack. The Task Force decided to go to Pearl Harbor to fuel up and replenish for a long trip.

We came into Pearl Harbor on the Sunday following the attack. The Harbor was in an incredible mess. There was six inches of oil on the water, fires still burning and ships aground. The inverted Arizona still had men living aboard unable to escape. Rumors were galore, for instance: a miniature suicide submarine was tied up under the hospital ship; A Japanese pilot who was shot down was trying to get into the population wearing the University of Oregon Letter sweater and speaking English; The Japanese had landed on the northern end of Oahu.

A pilot told me the following story prefacing it by saying that there were certain impolite words in the story, that are so accurate that there was really no substitute for them. This is how the story went. The pilot was from the USS Enterprise, scheduled to land in Hawaii on December 7th. Ordinarily on weekends, carriers let their pilots and crews fly in ahead of time to Oahu to get a head start on the parties that follow.

He had taken off from the Enterprise and was coming in over Oahu. Suddenly he noticed a strange new plane with a big red circle on each wing that he had never seen before, flying right beside him. He looked at the pilot who seemed oriental and waved at him. The pilot smiled back with an expression like a cat eating shit. Suddenly, the plane disappeared and he heard a tic, tic, tic, on his right wing, then a tic, tic, tic, on his left wing. He noticed bullet holes that he had never seen before and suddenly realized that the plane directly behind him was so close that the two lines of fire from his wing guns did not converge. If he increased his distance from this hostile plane he would be wiped out. Then there was a thump, thump, thump, from his gunner hitting the back of his cockpit in a panic. His gunner was shouting, "Mr. Crease, he is shooting real bullets at us!" Crease yelled back "Throw anything you can at him!"

The gunner and the pilot had not been very tidy in taking care of their plane, which was at present unarmed. Fortunately they had left a chain of tracer bullets lying around and the gunner found these. He put them in his machine gun and started firing a steady stream of these tracer bullets at the enemy plane. Tracer bullets are not explosive but the Japanese pilot knowing that Americans usually used one tracer bullet between many regular bullets probably assumed that he was being fired at by a super gun and pealed off.

The Japanese had mistaken the USS Idaho, a target ship covered with heavy oak planks, for the Lexington. A Target Ship is used for dive-bombers as target practice. Pilots drop bombs full of chalk dust, which burst on hitting the ship without harming it, while the Target Ship is taking evasive action. This ship, the Idaho, was torpedoed in the attack and immediately turned upside down. The Japanese who had an extensive observation organization mistakenly reported that the Lexington had been sunk.

The US Navy wanted the families of the Lexington crewmembers to be notified that they were OK and were in fact not sunk, without informing the Japanese of their mistake. The

Navy printed thousands of postcards, and gave them to the crewmembers. The postcards were preprinted with;

"Dear _ _ _,"

A multiple-choice section followed:

"_ I am well."

"_ I have survived."

"_ I am wounded." etc. They checked off the ones that applied. The name of their vessel was not given. Thus the crew's families were notified of their safety, without the Japanese finding out.

Now that the War had started there was no more discussion about whether or not it would, and we were too busy to think about dancing and parties.

The Battle of the Coral Sea

The following is my account of my experiences during the battle and its aftermath. For a detailed description of the military activities during this battle check with Google asking for USS Lexington CV 2. The pictures are from Google.

The battle started for me on May 7, 1942 when I was 23 years old. My roommate, who was a dive-bomber, had just returned from an attack on a Japanese fleet in the Coral Sea. He told us about the sinking of a small Japanese aircraft carrier, the Shoshone. The American forces made a classic attack: dive bombers coming down from on high and torpedo planes coming in low on each side, all simultaneously. The carrier could not concentrate its antiaircraft fire. Our squadron leader's 1000-pound bomb knocked planes off the Shoshone's flight deck and our torpedo planes nearly blew off the ship's bottom. My roommate said the Shoshone went under water about 20 minutes after the first bomb hit. None of the crew could have escaped; they did not have a chance. Our reaction was, "Those poor guys. They were out here just like us, fighting for their country."

After my roommate's accounts, he always gave us a bottle of pop of which he had a drawer full. After he told us the report of this attack he gave us all a second soda pop, saying, "It could be us tomorrow, so there is no point in having it go to waste".

The USS Lexington, CV 2 was authorized in 1916 as a battle cruiser. It was placed on hold, laid down on January 1921, suspended through February 1922, redesigned and reauthorized as an aircraft carrier in July 1922, launched in 1925, and finally commissioned on 14 December 1927, nine years after it was originally authorized. This drawn out time period caused plenty of room for error.

It was 888 feet long, and weighed 36,000 long tons. By 1942 it had 100 officers, by 1840 it had an aviation group of

141 officers and 710 enlisted men. Her flight deck was 866 feet long and up to 105 feet wide. Her hangar was the largest single enclosed space on any ship with an area of 73,528 square feet. The forward elevator was 30 by 60 feet and the after elevator was 30 by 36 feet.

Two in-line engine rooms powered the ship, each containing a steam turbine driven generator. Steam came from 16 boilers, each in their own room. There were four boiler rooms on each side of each engine room. The electricity they made to drive the ship went to the motor rooms, one for each of the four propellers. For each propeller there were two motors. These were about 20 feet in diameter; 22 or 44 poles could be used. Six motor-generators provided electricity for use on the ship.

The ship was designed to reach 33.25 knots (38.26mph) but actually made 34.59 knots.

The engine room's power was staggering. From December 17, 1929 until January 16, 1930 it supplied power to the city of Tacoma, Washington, when the city dam ran out of water. The city would not have had power until its dam's reservoir refilled.

The USS Lexington was moored to the city dock, and was connected to Tacoma's electrical grid to keep the city running. The boilers were cut in and out as needed.

The rating required by the disarmament treaty, when the ship was built, was limited to 30,000-horse power and it had never used more. During the ship's last few hours, the Chief Engineer, who knew the ship was doomed, wanted to find out what the ship's capacity really was. He maximized at 50,000-horse power.

The Water Main.

The major water main carried salt water for all purposes and extended completely around the ship, just inboard of the boiler rooms. The forward and after sections of the fire main were separated by valves.

My Battle Station

Every morning we had a routine bugle call to send us to our General Quarters. This meant that everyone went to their own assigned battle station to prepare for prospective battle conditions.

My battle station was below the armored hangar deck and just above the entrance to the After Engine Room. I was in charge of the After Engineering Repair Party. It was composed of 18 members of the Engineering Department and all skills were represented. I had been acquainting myself with the after part of the ship during routine General Quarters, insuring that all the fire hoses were good and learning the locations of the leads to them.

The First Lieutenant

We were under the command of the First Lieutenant, Commander Healy, who was 3rd in command of the ship. His battle station was Central Station, which was low and forward. If the bridge was blown away, Central Station could take over and the vessel could be run from there. All controls of the Engine Rooms, communication and navigation could also be handled there. Commander Healy was in overall charge of damage control.

Internal Communications

We communicated by sound powered telephones. These contained superb magnets that used the energy of the voice, speaking into it to activate the earpieces of the receiver. No other power was needed.

We are attacked

Shortly after 9 AM, May 8, 1942, our planes went out to continue the battle. We were attacked by aircraft shortly after 11AM. We received bombs on the flight deck and a torpedo on the forward port quarter. (My memory of some details differ slightly from those related in Stanley Johnson's, "Queen of the Flat Tops.") The hole in the flight deck was quickly repaired, but the hole caused by the torpedo was ignored, because it did not seriously affect our speed or operation. One of the large bombs on the flight deck knocked out an anti-aircraft battery.

Big Damage

Things quieted down, but at 12:47 PM there was an explosion forward that sounded like a 5-inch gun going off. We had not received word of another attack.

It was getting into the afternoon and I had wanted to get some food for my crew. General Quarters had been sounded during breakfast and so some of them had not eaten yet. To send a man up to the galley for sandwiches would break watertight integrity, so I needed Pop Healy's permission. I called Central Station. No answer. I was about to send a man forward to Central Station to ask permission when the Chief Engineer came up out of the After Engine Room and ordered me to take my crew up to Central Station and help the Forward Engineering Repair Party.

We progressed forward. On the way we noticed that Fire Room Number 1 was flooded as a result of the torpedo hit. We were also told that the water main had been broken at the 1st valve, close by. Although we did not know it at the time, this was the ship's fatal wound, one that we should have tried to fix right away.

We arrived at the Forward Elevator Pit, closing the doors behind us. We found the remnants of the Forward Engineering Repair Party, completely exhausted. The access to Central Station was through a door in the floor of the pit. In the door there was a manhole, which was closed tightly. I opened the manhole and smoke came out. The Central Station personnel were down there. Obviously, we had to get them out right away. I could not send my men down into a place that I did not understand. With oxygen breathing apparatus I went through the manhole and down the ladder into the Forward Electrical Distribution Room. The lights were still working. The rail, guarding the forward switchboard was broken and the door into Central Station was open. Looking through I could see many men lying on the floor. The air smelled of toxic gas. We had to get them all out immediately. I put an unconscious friend over my shoulder and carried him to the manhole in the Forward Elevator Pit. He was grabbed from above and carried away by others. My oxygen breathing apparatus did not work and I had done all of this on practically one breath. I was exhausted, but knew that each of my men could manage to go into Central Station at least once. Together we pulled out about 20 crewmembers.

Flash Burns

I learned later that one of the Chief Petty Officers of my Division had been standing in the forward open doorway of Central Station when the blast occurred. The fiery blast knocked him down and nearly out. He said that he felt like lying down and resting but realized it could have been fatal to do so. With all the strength that he had, he pulled himself together and climbed out the way I had come in. His shirt had been open, and his chest looked like a baked turkey. He had had a flash burn. These peculiar burns are only skin-deep. A silk shirt covering would be sufficient protection against one. He recovered easily.

My Division Officer

My Division Officer's battle station was the Forward Electrical Distribution Room. He told me later the blast had come through the open door from Central Station, knocking him against the Board's protective rail and breaking it. His description of the appearance of the blast coming through the door with it's instantaneous blue sparks, reminded me of movies I had seen showing the gasoline explosions in the inside of an internal combustion engine.

Fire Fighting

After we had all recovered we set about fighting the fires, but because of the broken   main we had no water. I felt that it would be possible to contain the fire by shutting the watertight doors and sealing it off from the rest of the ship. We set about to do this.

I was called to the bridge to explain my situation. When I returned I found that several explosions had killed a number of my men. Recruiting others, we continued and had the fire isolated. The fire was burning on the other side of a bulkhead. But in those days they painted ships generously with oil-based paint, putting on red lead primer. Over the years the paint had built up to a quarter of an inch or more in thickness. It was rich in oils, and burned fiercely. I watched a bulkhead on which the paint was burning on the far side. It turned black and burst into flames. In the meantime minor explosions were occurring. We had to have water. There was water pressure in the after half of the ship. I sent two men aft with hoses to connect up to an after fireplug. In the meantime we kept trying to seal compartments.

Dilemma

After an hour and a half there was still no water. I followed the hose aft to see what the trouble was. Fire had burned through the electrical cables, the lights had gone out and so I used a battle lantern. I found my man, trying to attach the hose to a dripping fireplug. His hands were shaking and he was not able to make the connection. "Would you like me to do that?" I asked. "I wish you would, sir," he replied. He held the battle lantern while I sat down, but even without shaking I was also unable to make a connection. I tried for about 15 minutes.

Hopelessness

Then, another man came by and told us that we had orders to abandon ship. I could see that without water, fighting the fires, which were burning their way through the ship, was hopeless. All three of us went to the flight deck. The effort made to notify all hands to abandon ship was successful except for two who were unable to leave. These two were called on the sound powered telephone. They replied that they were low in the ship and completely surrounded by water. To open the watertight doors would flood them immediately. One of them replied, "You guys go and do your thing. We have a hell of an Acey-Deucy game going on down here, so don't bother us anymore."

Abandoning Ship

On the flight deck I met the Executive Officer; he said, "You are a scientist. Can you tell me how hot the torpedoes can get before they explode?" (We were standing right over them.) I replied, "The explosive is torpex and it's melting point is 180°F. They are set off only by percussion." The torpedoes were above the hangar deck and getting pretty hot. The flight deck was quite crowded with the 2500 plus crew members who were waiting to get off. The life rafts had been lowered 70 feet to the ocean's surface. To reach them we were to go down a knotted rope. It would not be good to have too many people in the water close to the ship at one time, so we had to be patient.

A destroyer came alongside and took off the wounded. This worked well.

The rest of us just hung around, as if reluctant to leave. I put my automatic and my cap into an airplane on the flight deck, expecting to pick them up when we returned after the ship had burnt out. It was late in the afternoon and most had not eaten. The caretaker for the ship's soda fountain had been killed in the air attack. No one was minding the store. Helpful souls gathered the ice cream in its big containers with scoops and brought them out on deck. Others brought cups, small plastic spoons and the condiments to make up a variety of Sundays. They were quite generous and patient and there were no charges. We could have all we wanted. At this particular time it was especially good.

Going Down and Out

Taking off my shoes and denim shirt, I went down over the side. The life raft, which I reached, was full of men, each paddling in their own direction. If we had one person in charge, we could have all the men paddle together to get away from the ship. My rank identification was gone, so I suggested to the crowd that the largest man would be our skipper and would direct us. The crowd bought this and we paddled away from the ship. The ship was drifting downwind sideways and a horizontal whirlpool brought us back to the overhanging sponson. We tried going off the stern of the ship but a vertical whirlpool brought us back again. After that, discipline broke down.

Someone on the flight deck had thrown an airplane's two-man rubber life raft over the side and it drifted by empty. "This is for me," I thought, and shedding everything except my boxer shorts, I went for it. By the time I reached the raft there were four others with it, including a wounded aviator. I suggested he become skipper in the raft, while each of us outside in the water, could hold a corner and paddle away from the ship, with our other arm, as directed by him, This worked very well. It was a beautiful day, 85°F, deep blue water, white-caps and 15 foot waves.

Escape

Three destroyers and two cruisers were circling the Lexington in about a five-mile radius. Each sent out its single motor whaleboat to pick us up, the smaller whaleboats from the destroyers collected the ones nearest to them first. The larger whaleboats from the cruisers towed the large life rafts away from the ship. A small motor whaleboat came along with only three empty spaces. The coxswain would not leave 2 of us out there alone, so he took us all aboard. This meant we had only three inches of freeboard left on each side, leaving us little room to maneuver in these big waves. We had two bailers removing water that we took on board.

Photo # 80-G-16664   Large explosion on board USS Lexington, Battle of the Coral Sea

All went well with us in the motor whaleboat until the Lexington blew up. There was much debris in the air. A piece of deck about 15 feet square came at us. The coxswain could ordinarily have avoided it but his limited freeboard made that very difficult. When the 'would-be lethal fragment' was about two thirds of it's way to us, the wind caught it and it veered slightly, hitting the water nearby. We continued on to a destroyer and climbed up the rope netting they had dropped over the side for us.

Goodbye and transfer

My time with the Lexington was over. I was completely exhausted; they escorted me to a bunk. I slept for a day or two without being aware of what was going on around me.

The people on the destroyer were very kind. One Marine gave me a pair of trousers, another a shirt with a single ensign caller bar and another a set of underwear. I was told later that on the Lexington there had been many more big explosions and that flames from burning gasoline and fuel oil soared hundreds of feet high. The Lexington and the Yorktown were the only two carriers we had in that part of the Pacific against Japan's forty. All the uninjured pilots and undamaged aircraft had been transferred to the Yorktown, seriously augmenting their power.

Photo # NH 51382   USS Lexington burning during the Battle of Coral Sea, May 1942

The Yorktown was now the only functional U.S. carrier in the southwest Pacific. For strategic reasons the Navy did not want the Japanese to not know that the Lexington was no longer a threat to them. They also did not want the Japanese to capture it and take any information off the ship. It was important to keep them uninformed. Therefore one of our destroyers, USS Phelps, was dispatched and put two torpedoes into each side of the Lexington, sinking her.

For the crew of the Lexington this was very sad because we all loved the ship. My personal losses were my clothes, my notes and among other things, the Naval Sword on which my name had been engraved.

I heard three stories about Captain Sherman's departure from the ship. Here is the one that I liked the best, from the man who picked him up. Captain Sherman delayed his departure until he was sure that all hands were off the ship. He was about to descend the rope from a sponson, which was overhung by the after starboard quarter of the flight deck, with the Executive Officer, when the explosion occurred. He said to the Executive Officer, "Let's stand under this piece of the flight deck until the debris quits falling out of the sky," and then he called down to the coxswain of the rescue boat to get close to the ship under its overhang. After the sky was clear, they descended.

Captain Sherman was made an Admiral later during the War. Another brother invented the Sherman tank used by the Allies in Europe. Another was Superintendent of Schools in my hometown; Andover MA and I became well acquainted with him when we were both camp counselors at Camp Winnicook. His mother must have been very proud of her sons.

A Happy Ship.

The Lexington had been a happy ship. Early in its history there had been a vast poker game. Each crewmember had put in $5 and as the games progressed the money became concentrated in the hands of the best players. This was quite illegal, of course. The Captain let it go until the last game, and then he walked in and picked up $5,000 that was on the table. He took this $5,000 and used it for a party for the whole ship's company. He rented a hotel, and hired a fine big band. Everyone had such a wonderful time. A committee was formed to manage the party. We were each charged $5 and the money went towards another party the following year and each year thereafter. I attended the last one in a big hotel on Waikiki Beach. It was fabulous.

Noumea, capitol of the French colony of New Caledonia had a magnificent roadstead. There were many ships in this even though, at that time, we were not sure whether the government was Free French or Nazi French.

To keep the loss of the Lexington a secret for strategic reasons required that over 2500 survivors not tell anybody. No way could the secret be kept if we all got ashore. We were transferred to three troop transports which meant there were well over 300 men in each, plus crew. These three ships were ordered to go south and anchor in a roadstead off Tongatapu, with no way to communicate with anyone, except by censored mail. We stayed there past the decisive Battle of Midway.

Off Tongatapu

Spending several months aboard these transport ships provided a good time to catch up on our sleep and find ingenious ways to kill time. The crews of the transports had only a few personal books. They kindly shared these with us and they were read to shreds. Each of the three ships had a single motor whaleboat. These they used to transport groups of us to Tongatapu, where we could walk on land. The queen of the islands had wisely moved all females from ages six to sixty to another island, leaving not much to do there, except walk.

<u>Tongatapu</u>.

I had to wait my turn to get there. When my turn finally came we landed on a simple beach. I crossed the beach and came to a gravel road. This was my first walk on land in about 150 days. It was very nice. About four miles down that road I came across an anomaly, an English bungalow with a white picket fence, a nicely cut lawn and flowerbeds. I stood by the fence and looked at it. It had windows, but no glass was in them. Beautiful music of a strange quality was coming out of one of the windows. It had to be a clavichord, the predecessor of the piano. Although I had never heard one before, I had had it described to me. I stood there listening. A very elderly woman came to the window. She asked me what I was doing. I told her that I was listening to the music and asked her if it was a clavichord she was playing. She said it was. She told me her father had been a missionary there and had brought it to the island. She herself was born and raised on Tongatapu, educated in England and returned there to live as the wife of a younger missionary. I thanked her for the information and she invited me in for tea. I could not accept, because I was due back in just a little over an hour and did not want to miss my boat. She went back to her playing...

Baa, baa, black sheep
Have you any wool?
Yes Sir, yes sir,
Three bags full,

One for my Master,
One for my Dame,
And one for the little boy
Who lives down the lane.

On the way back to the boat landing I came to a tent. In it was a Tongan soldier. I asked him where I could buy some tapa cloth. He told me that those who had come before me had bought all that was on the island. I noticed that the ground padding for his blanket roll was a piece of tapa cloth. "Would you sell me that piece?" I asked.

" Oh that's no good." he said, "My little sister just made that to practice her designs."

I said "$15 is all I have," and I gave it to him saying, "I may not be this way again."

"You are very generous," he said, "I'll throw in a lauhala mat."

This woven mat was large enough to have a picnic on and when it was folded it would not crease, but would remain flexible.

I returned to my boat in time and thus ended my first visit to a beautiful South Sea island with a mat and a piece of tapa cloth which I have to this day.

The Mismatch

My only work during this period was the recording of my experiences during the battle. Many of us were doing this. The most interesting thing I learned was from an old Chief Petty Officer. He had been assigned to the Lexington before it was commissioned, while it was still being converted from a battle cruiser to an aircraft carrier.

He told me that the threads of the fireplugs and fire hoses in the forward part of the ship did not match those in the after part of the ship. Had I known this, I would have taken hoses from the after part of the ship to bring the water forward to fight the fires. For want of the right hose, possibly, a ship was lost. Pop Healy may have known this, but he was killed before I needed to know.

Amusement

There was not much to do for amusement on the vessels, mainly just books to read, and a chance to go for a walk. However, we did come up with a rather interesting and time-consuming hobby. A small group of us had a contest to see who could develop the deepest tan. Another fellow and I became quite dark and looked rather flashy with our blue eyes, white teeth and our deep mahogany faces. Constant exposure to the sun close to the equator will do that. When we returned to Hawaii, we lost about a third of our tan, even sunbathing constantly for a week at Pearl Harbor, while the ship replenished its supplies. We had hoped to bring this deep tan with us to San Diego.

Recovery

We arrived in San Diego in July and I visited the friend whom I had carried out of Central Station in early May. He was still in the hospital and had recovered physically but not mentally. He was sitting up in bed when I visited. His wife was there. He was very alert and was working with a clipboard in his lap. He had just proudly written down, "Tuesday." He asked me if I was from the Lexington and how to spell my name which he wrote down.

His wife told me that he had been taken from the Lexington by a destroyer and eventually flown to San Diego. He had been unconscious for several weeks. His body had not been badly damaged and had fully recovered physically, but carbon monoxide had damaged his brain. His wife said that he had recovered much and would recover more but it was unlikely he would recover completely. I wished them well and left. I was glad that I had made the visit but felt sorry that I couldn't help in any way.

Living

The Navy is very careful with its people and likes to plan each career. Imagine the amount of work when 2500 of us were dumped on them in San Diego with no ship. It also took some time to get us all properly in uniforms.

The officers were stationed at the Bachelor Officers Quarters on Coronado Island, off San Diego Bay. This was a source of great delight to the Navy juniors, who were the daughters of officers stationed on Coronado Island. Nearly all the eligible suitors were off fighting a war. So our presence there was appreciated. I remember lying on my back beside the swimming pool with my head in a luscious lap, fingers stroking my hair, and lovely hands pouring martinis into my mouth.

"What Ship are you on?" she would ask.

"The USS Lexington." I would answer.

"And where is the Lexington?" she would ask.

In a dispirited way, I would wave my hand and say, "She's out there."

She would pour some more martini into my mouth, stroke my hair again and say, "Oh you poor, poor dear."

I looked at a surviving buddy who was several feet away, also with his head in an equally hospitable lap and sipping a handheld martini. He looked at me and said, "Rocky, War is Hell, isn't it!"

Dancing

My best time for dancing was about 1943 in San Diego. At the time I was the Electrical Officer of a small aircraft carrier. Our ship was in the Navy yard for an overhaul for a month and a half. The crew had every other night ashore. Two of my friends had cars and would bring everyone to where we all were dancing. Before picking me up they would pick up this particular woman. She was about my height, willowy and athletic, with dark eyes and light brown hair. She would not tell me her name nor would my friends. I surmised that she was the wife of a pilot missing in action. I did not press. A woman in this situation would be socially limited but she could dance with me.

This was the time of the big bands, the Big Apple, the shag and the birth of swing. Our favorite step was the very simple, but vigorous shag. It started with two bounces the left foot, then two bounces on the right, followed by one on the left and one on the right, kicking out slightly in each case. The beauty of it was that, with the right music, you could do about everything, such as run, go forwards, back, sideways, slurp, shoulder toss, lift your partner with both hands, hold her up, and not miss a beat. Two athletic people doing this together for any length of time could get pretty good. Whenever we went dancing my dark eyed friend and I sought each other out. But all good things come to an end, in this case very reluctantly.

At our last dance each of our group knew that we would never all be together again. So we went from our regular spot to an after hours place. When that closed we went to an after, after, hours place. We finally wound up in the Palladium, which did not serve liquor, so we just danced to Tommy Dorsey's big band. There were about two thousand dancers there, in that huge hall. My partner said, "Let's go!" and so we started in. The music, of course was superb. We did it all. Near the end of the dance we broke apart. Two people doing this fast step appear to be floating. She floated around me, and I floated around her maintaining eye contact. She reached up with one hand over her head. I reached up and took her hand. She twirled three times, skirt flaring. I stepped forward and grabbed her by the waist. We ran 20 feet. We stopped. She tilted back, arms out-stretched till her hair was touching the floor. Then I snapped her back over my shoulder, grabbed her by the hips with both hands and held her high, never missing a beat or loosing eye contact. I set her down. The music stopped at 6 AM. There we were in the center of a clear circle with a 40-foot radius. Officer's whites looked good for this. Everyone was clapping. We were embarrassed. It was time to leave if I was to get back to my ship on time.

I had to go to work, immediately on returning to the ship, at 7AM. I had my men overseeing each navy yard project to insure it was done satisfactorily. As I went down the list and assigned a man to check each item, I was greeted with a remarkably enthusiastic, "Yes Sir!" After all was assigned, and only the Chief Petty Officer and I were left, I said "Chief, the men seemed so especially respectful, today." He replied, "Oh sir, you should have seen yourself last night!"

I happily noticed that all the poor electrical workmanship was caught and corrected before we left port.

So perhaps another page in Naval Leadership needs to be written.

The Sexual Behavior of the Male Red Salmon

In 1947 the Alaska Salmon Industry learned that they could catch male and female salmon differentially. Thinking about their slogan, "Fish in the Can," led them to wonder if they could catch more males than females without hurting the spawning.

Accordingly, they made a contract with the University of Washington Fisheries Research Institute to determine how important male salmon are in salmon production. The University, in its wisdom, had a group of men observe the behavior of male salmon.

I was very fortunate to have been called up for one month to help with this project. I was flown in to the west end of Lake Nerka where the Institute had built a cabin. Lake Nerka is the second of the five Wood River lakes north of Dillingham, Alaska, on Bristol Bay.

There, I was given a large pack of food for the camp and a skiff to cross a small bay to the mouth of Pick Creek. After securing the skiff, I walked two miles up the creek on a well-defined trail over a tree-less tundra. The creek flowed from a number of springs. The springs were like large ponds about a tenth of an acre to one acre in size. The ponds had gravel bottoms. The water coming out of the gravel was 36 degrees F. and flowed constantly all year round. The camp consisted of a large tent with cots and a fireplace some distance away.

There were about eight men on the team. Those coming up from the cabin would bring food, etc. We watched the salmon during daylight hours and slept for the very few hours when it was too dark to see them. We took turns to watch the salmon. When it was our turn we carried our trash to the cabin, caught up on sleep, washed, reviewed our notes and did tasks to keep the camp running.

We were observing the behavior of about fifty marked males. I was given a couple of days to look at the various salmon. I found that there were amazing differences in their individual behavior. Each male salmon seemed to have its own personality.

Before coming up I had scoured the available literature for information on the spawning procedures of the salmon family members. I found only one detailed description. It said that the female makes a nest, lays her eggs, and then the male swims over the nest and fertilizes the eggs.

Our 50 male salmon had been marked with large colored tags. Various team members were assigned to watch particular males and record their behavior. I was told to spend a day looking at the different fish to get an idea about what was going on, but I was warned not to name the salmon after any of my friends. The behavior of each male was very different from the others and there seemed to be no general rules. I was assigned one salmon that had a bright green tag. This fish did not court females but simply waited until a nest was ready and then dashed in, pushed the courting male aside and fertilized the eggs.

My fish was watching a courting pair building a nest. I was lucky. The nest was being built right next to a tussock. The tussock was an 18 inch high tuft of grass and earth growing out of the water. It was about 3 feet long and 2 feet wide with vertical sides. In picking a spawning site, the male picks the best area he can get and within that area the female picks her spot to dig. Their site was about 18 inches from my head as I lay on the adjacent bank looking through the grass. The water was about 3 inches deep so the salmon swam half out of the water. My fish, the intruder that I was watching was about 6 to 8 feet to my right and waiting.

The female moved about 6 to 8 times her body volume of gravel in two and and a half hours. This was a lot of work. She appeared to get tired and discouraged. The male cruised around, mostly checking on other males and keeping apprised of her situation. When he saw that the female's fins were drooping, he would come over and encourage her. While she was at the bottom of the nest he would swim over her rubbing his body over her adipose fin. She would freeze and tiny waves would radiate out from her sides. You could almost feel her very low subsonic sigh. She would then do the same to him. These caresses were repeated several times by each. After which she would sparkle and start digging again with vigor.

My problem was to maintain 100% focus for 2 1/2 hours. The sex act lasts only 5 to 6 seconds and it is very easy to miss it. We had found that the best way to maintain this level of attention was to take notes and to record every move that each salmon made. This we did using a stopwatch and a clipboard. The beating of the tail of the female was a good indicator of the readiness to spawn.

The task of the female salmon was to create a bed 6 or more inches below the original level of the gravel. It had to be made so that the vents of both the male and female salmon would be directly over the only opening into the gravel pocket into which the eggs would fall. As the nest neared completion the male would frequently try it for size and shape. Then the female would correct deficiencies. While this was going on the would-be intruder became more alert and more ready to dart in.

While progress generally ran smoothly, interruptions did sometimes happen. One instance was when an old male got into the nest. The female appeared very upset and dashed to her mate. "There is someone in our nest," she seemed to say, pointing with her little fin. He dashed over and beat the daylights out of the intruder. However, the intruder was old and feeble and was unable to get out of the nest's depression. Noticing this the male took a pectoral fin of the feeble intruder in his mouth, and pushed the visitor's nose into the tussock. Then he went back, grabbed the tail fin and pushed that to the edge of the nest. Returning to the pectoral fin he pulled the fish away from the tussock and shoved it in again about 6 inches further on. In this way he moved the visitor out of the nest, a quarter of the way around the tussock and into the nest of another pair where that male beat the daylights out of him again.

After watching salmon spawn a number of times, one can pretty well anticipate when the nest is ready. In this case the male came in and lay with the female and I could see that there was a rock out of place. I thought, "No, not yet." She corrected the error. He came back and lay there. "Now," I thought. The male froze. The green-tagged fish that I was assigned to was a would-be interloper. He had moved up slightly in the direction of the nest. The male rushed out into the shallow, 3-inch deep water, grabbed the would-be intruder by the petrol fin, hitting him on the side, and knocking him over. Still holding on to the pectoral fin but now on top of the would-be intruder and completely out of the water he brought his entire weight up and then down on the other male, rapidly again and again for almost half a minute. The attacked fish did not move for nearly 20 minutes.

The male then returned to the nest. He lay with his female, their mouths were open, their bodies tilted so that their vents almost touched, and they both pushed. The eggs came out in a steady stream about 3 diameters apart, and went directly down into the pocket in the rocks made for them. The milt from the male, a slender white stream about the size of a pencil lead came out and was directed to the descending stream of eggs. It completely surrounded each egg as it went into the small, less than an inch in diameter, hole. The stream of eggs was steady and stopped when the pocket was full. No eggs were spilled. It was a beautiful event in both timing and quality. The male went off; the female went into an ecstatic dance in the form of a figure 8 on its side. At each turn she would flip a rock over the hole where the eggs were buried. The largest rocks were put in first.

There were experiments. One was where a single male was put in a large cage with 30 females. Each had plenty of room. He started out by dutifully courting one and then another. But he soon realized that he did not have time for such niceties and began to take his responsibilities more seriously. They were all making nests for him. He would try one out; if it fit he would spawn, if not he would move on. In one interesting situation, he passed over one female 4 times and each time he moved on to the same next one and spawned with her. On the 4th time the one who was passed by, darted out hitting her neighbor on the side and knocked her clear out of the spawning nest right during the spawning act. Eggs were scattered all over and exposed to the lethal sunlight.

Although the male seemed to spawn with most of the females, only half of the eggs were fertilized. The explanation seemed to be that he was spawning faster than his gonads were ripening. Apparently, males were not built for steady spawning. This had been anticipated by the program designers and in a further experiment, two males were put in with 30 females. Oddly, the results were about the same because the 2 males spent most of their time fighting over a single female, and neglected some of the others. This puzzled us and we tried to figure out in a special staff meeting what that female had that the others lacked. All we could agree on was that that female was an especially cute little salmon.

There were two other experiments, the Monks and the Nuns. Five males were placed in a small cage without any females. They spent their entire time trying to get out and died with faces quite raw from trying to push through the chicken wire. Five females were similarly isolated without males. They just spent their time digging nests. One made a nest a foot and a half deep and finally laid her eggs in it. Some of the others also deposited eggs. None of these eggs, of course, developed.

I also observed the fish in a natural area. The area chosen was a small bay about 100 feet across on the west side of the main stream. It was gridded by white string so that the locations of the 4 marked males could be recorded. The males were located at the points of a large triangle with one in the center. All the males had females.

The pair at the top of the triangle at the north end of the pool were very devoted to each other. The male would drive away other females and the female would drive away other males. They stayed together until she was spawned out and then she drove him away to greener pastures. Spawned out females do not like to have other salmon near where their eggs have been buried.

The male in the southwest corner loved to fight. He would not wait to be challenged but would simply attack any other male except his close neighbors. He was good at it and he knew all the holds. He kept his corner pretty well cleared out. Interestingly, his mate helped him fight. She would swim around and entice another male into their nest and then dart over to her male, pointing with her little fin as if to say, "There is a stranger in our nest!" The male would then dart over and beat the daylights out of the intruder.

The male in the Southeast corner was an even better fighter who never lost. Being next to the main stream, there were plenty of males going by. He prevented the interloper type of salmon from entering the bay. He needed no help from his female.

In the middle of the triangle there was a male with two females. Since it takes about 2 1/2 hours to build a nest and spawn, he had them spaced 1 1/4 hours apart. He devoted his entire attention to them. When a wandering male happened by, he would not fight but would escort the intruder to one of the two fighters and let them do it. He died without a mark on his body!

The Alaska salmon industry in Bristol Bay was managed by a number of canneries. These provided small sailing whale-boats and nets to the fishermen. The season lasted from late June to about the middle of August. The managers of these canneries were generally not owners but rather men who had worked their way up from the bottom. They were a hard and tough lot having had to manage members of the world's oldest industry without much law enforcement (he had to give her a fish). They had to know and handle all the tricks of this ancient trade. All of them had worked several decades in the Bristol Bay salmon fishery, but none of them had ever seen salmon spawn. Of course they knew that salmon did spawn. Being the end of the season, they all got together and rented two Norseman (large single-engine float planes that carry 9 passengers each). With these they flew to the mouth of the creek and walked the two miles to our working area. They wanted to see some salmon spawn. My boss and friend, Ole, asked me to take over explaining the mating process as it progressed.

It was not an easy task. It would be relatively easy to show 2 or 3 people but 20, was a different story. The best place I could find in the time available was a spot alongside a section of the stream draining the springs. At a bend in the stream the bank on the outside of the bend was about 6 feet high. Fortunately, the bank slopes steeply to the stream in a series of steps, which made an ideal amphitheater.

The stream itself was poor the rocks being relatively large. A pair of small salmon would be spawning in about 20 minutes. This was the best I could find. The little female dug valiantly. The little male was especially attentive and gave her maximum support, encouraging her greatly. I stood downstream from them and explained what was going on. Then something happened that I had never seen before. The female, in question was trying to remove an intruding rock. She had removed all the gravel around it and had made it quite loose. But she could not get it out of the way. Finally, she was trying to push it with her nose. With each push it moved a little. Then the male dropped over alongside her and started to push with her. I looked over at the audience. To my horror they were all shifting their shoulders with each push, each giving all the moral support they could. They were involved. I knew something terrible was going to happen because at my heels a lone male was approaching. I went over to the audience's side of the stream. The pair was ready to spawn and opened their mouths to push. The intruder dashed in, pushed the little male aside and let out a big white cloud of milt.

BANG, BANG – BANG, BANG, BANG, -- "THAT S.O.B. WILL NEVER DO THAT AGAIN!" said the shooter as he shoved his automatic back into its holster.

The intruder drifted down the stream, three bullet holes in it's side, and blood coming out of it's mouth. The male tried to get back but it was too late. The eggs were gone and many were scattered. The audience got up and each wandered off quietly in a different direction. No one is going to laugh at a man who can hit a submerged salmon in a running stream three out of five times.

Mothers' Day

We all celebrate Mother's day in our own way. Mother's day was coming up and my friend Ann wrote me an email in which she suggested that I think of my mother. I sent one back to her with the following, as part of the answer: You asked me to think of my mom and I did.

My mother was very sociable, and worked her way into the near upper crust, of which she selected 'nice' people as friends. I have a number of total recalls of interesting incidents. Here is the most interesting:

I had come up from Washington, D.C. to see my mother for the last time and to say good-bye. She was in a hospital in Lawrence, Massachusetts. She knew that she was dying but had the strength to hold off until after my visit. Mother was overjoyed when I came into her private room, saying that she was so glad that I had come. She then proceeded, very proudly, to introduce me to her friends. Apparently, my mother saw her friends coming to meet me in a line. I could not see them, but she could. I had known most of them, and felt very strongly that they were in the room with us. Most of them had died. She had had many older friends that she always liked to look after. Confused, I made appropriate replies such as; "Oh yes, I remember you. When I was little, we saw you off on the Cunard Line Ship on your way to Europe."; "That was a lovely time we had at your house on Lake Sunapee, in New Hampshire"; "It was such fun for the family to visit you in Pittsfield," etc. All the while I was trying to be calm and cheerful. Then my mother interrupted herself saying, "Not you, oh Faceless One. Not yet, and my son is not ready for you!" She then went on calmly introducing the rest of her friends. After she was through, we said goodbye and then I left. She died shortly afterwards.

That last visit with my mother made quite an impression on me. I had dropped everything at short notice to come and see her. She demonstrated how proud she was of me by introducing me to all her friends. We each had a thousand things to say, but all we could convey was the strong love we had for each other. Really, that was all that mattered.

It is good to look back in our lives and remember. We often go through life, one incident after another, too busy to give them much thought. But how we react to an incident determines who we are and what we become. At the time, an incident may seem curious or trivial. However, later our response to it may take on a deeper meaning. Without remembering or being reminded of it, an appreciation of its depth could be lost.

The Expendable Bathythermograph

I went to Washington DC in 1961, to coordinate the development of oceanographic instruments by government agencies that studied the oceans. This story explains part of my oceanographic instrumentation experience.

The US Navy had formed the Interagency Committee of Oceanography, chaired by Dr. James Wakeland, Assistant Secretary for Research and Development. The Committee had many panels, which were chaired by Bureau Chiefs. The chief of the Bureau of Commercial Fisheries, of which I was a member, chaired the Panel of Instrumentation, Facilities and Equipment. He was very busy running the Bureau and so left me to do most of the work. One of the panel's objectives was to encourage development of new equipment by the joint work of industrial and governmental laboratories. The expendable bathythermograph was one of the successful developments, which came out of this.

A bathythermograph is a device that will measure temperature versus depth, at any point in the ocean. In the ocean the top layer of water is warmer than water below. The temperature change between the two layers is abrupt and is known as the thermocline. The lower colder water is denser than the warmer water above. Because of this, debris, which cannot float on the lighter warmer water at high levels, can float below at the thermocline level where the water is denser. This creates a band of debris at the thermocline level. Knowledge of the location of the thermocline is important to fisheries because the tuna feed here. Fishermen can regulate the depth of their trawls accordingly.

In the denser and colder lower layer of water, sound travels much faster than in the warmer water above. Knowing the depth of the thermocline level is also very important to the

Navy, who use it in their acoustic methods of underwater echo sounding for submarine search.

The Bathythermograph was developed to locate the thermocline. This instrument was about a yard long and two inches thick. It was suspended from a cable over the side of a stationary vessel and could be lowered over a thousand feet. The data was recorded on a small glass slide, on which the relationship between depth and temperature were drawn. The Expendable Bathythermograph (EBT), made by Sipican could be used on a ship going at full speed. This was a great advantage to fishermen and Navy ships. Sipican was a small company near Cape Cod, Massachusetts.

Graham Campbell, from Sipican, came to me with an expendable bathythermograph. He said that its accuracy had been tested and verified in a mile-deep vertical mineshaft filled with water. The devise contained a spool of about two thousand feet of fine wire, which unpeeled as it fell. On the ship was a small box and graph maker that pealed out it's wire as the ship moved away from the dropping point. The cost of the devise to be dropped, plus the very fine cable was about twenty-five dollars. This was a devise that did not require the ship to change its speed. It was useful to fishermen, the Navy, oceanographers and weather people. Also the price was something that fishermen could afford.

Graham Campbell was interested in having the Bureau of Commercial Fisheries test the XBT, at sea. I arranged to use a vessel from our Washington DC Oceanographic Laboratory in an International Oceanographic observation, which was taking place in the Gulf of Africa, in 1965. There were already international expeditions studying oceanography here. Vessels from seven countries were researching a good location for a tuna fishery in the area. The tsetse fly had decimated cattle in Central Africa. A tuna fishery would augment the availability of fish protein for Central Africa. The U.S. Commercial Fisheries Laboratory of Washington DC, of which I was a part, was participating in this study. An expendable bathythermograph to locate the thermocline would be essential in this research.

Sipican loaned us their equipment and facilities, to determine the ground truth on how their expendable bathythermograph would work. We were acting as an independent party that had not been involved in its manufacture. We gathered much valuable data, using this equipment in the Gulf of Africa.

In the mean time General Motors had developed an expendable bathythermograph. It was spherical and about five inches in diameter. It cost about $300 each time it was used. Fishermen could not afford to pay that much. In the testing of this equipment, the rate of fall had been checked in a tank that was only ten feet deep. A team of researchers was sent over to my laboratory and tried to convince me that this G.M. model was superior to the Sipican one. Later an assistant to Senator Magnusson asked me to buy some and test them at sea. Sipican had given us hundreds of devises, which we disposed of in the Gulf of Africa; we could not afford to duplicate this trial. I did not see that the use of this devise was practical.

A former colleague, from the University of Washington's Applied Physics Laboratory, visited me. To my distress, he advised me to recommend the G.M. project over the Sipican project. I told him why I could not do that. He told me that if I did not, I would lose my Laboratory. I was rather shocked by this gross attempt at corruption by an academician from Seattle.

I thought of my great grandfather, the first Republican candidate for Governor of Massachusetts, for whom I was named. He had been offered the support of an extremist right-wing group similar to the John Birch Society. This was on condition that he dropped one plank in his platform, when he ran in 1836. If he had accepted their support, he would have won the election, but that plank, was to abolish slavery in Massachusetts. He pointed out that this was the reason he was running for Governor. So he lost the election. I knew what was morally proper in my current situation, so likewise, I lost my Laboratory!

The Navy does not like to have a sole source for anything they need a large number of. The Sipican patent on the Expendable Bathythermograph was a problem for them. They found a possible infringement on a patent belonging to Script's Oceanographic Institute. Having plenty of money, the Navy could afford to keep a lawsuit going until Sipican gave up and sold their patent to them for five million dollars.

Graham Campbell and I were planning to publish a book of our experience over this. The title of the book would be, 'How People in Government and Industry Can Work Together and Maintain Their Integrity'. The book was to be made up of perforated blank pages, which could be torn out. We would request that if the reader had any ideas they could just send them to us, because we couldn't think of any.

Unfortunately this book never came to fruition because soon after this incident Graham Campbell died and I was sent to Alaska.

Fin